The Art of Crochet for Beginners

Step By Step Visual Guide

Learn to Crochet Like a Pro in Less than a Week!

By

Katrina Gale

Copyrighted Material

Copyright © 2017 – **CSB Academy Publishing**

All rights reserved. In accordance with the U.S. Copyright Act of 1976, the scanning, uploading, and electronic sharing of any part of this book without the permission of the publisher is unlawful piracy and theft of the author's intellectual property. If you would like to use material from this book (other than for review purposes), prior written permission must be obtained by contacting the publisher. Thank you for your support of the author's rights.

CSB Academy Publishing Co.
P. O. Box 966
Semmes, Alabama 36575, USA

Cover Design & Illustration

By

Jane Keller

First Edition

Table of Contents

INTRODUCTION 5
CHAPTER 1 – ESSENTIAL EQUIPMENT 7
    5 Areas of a Crochet Hook 7
        Point 8
        Throat 8
        The Shaft 9
        The Thumb Rest 9
        The Handle 9
    Other Types of Crochet Hooks 11
    Choosing Your Yarn 11
        Crochet Abbreviations 17
CHAPTER 2 – GETTING STARTED 19
    4 Steps to a Slip Knot 19
    Holding the Hook 20
    Making a Chain 22
        Here is how to make a chain in crochet 22
    Which is the Right Side? 27
CHAPTER 3 – THE SINGLE CROCHET STITCH 30
    Working the Next Row (or Two) 36
CHAPTER 4 – DOUBLE CROCHET 40
    Double Crochet Row One 40
CHAPTER 5 – TREBLE CROCHET 48
    7 steps to make your first row of treble crochet 48
CHAPTER 5 – HALF DOUBLE CROCHET 55
    Here is how to make the half double crochet stitch 55
CHAPTER 6 – INCREASING AND DECREASING 60

4 Steps to Increasing in Single Crochet 60

5 steps to Double Crochet Increase 61

    Increasing in Treble Crochet 63

    Increasing in Half Double Crochet 63

4 Steps to Decreasing in Single Crochet 64

4 Steps to Decreasing in Double Crochet 65

12 Steps to Decreasing in Treble Crochet 67

6 Steps to Half Double Crochet Decrease 69

CHAPTER 7 – CHANGING COLORS AS YOU CROCHET 72

    Changing Colors in Single Crochet 72

    Changing Colors in Double Crochet 73

CHAPTER 8 – WORKING IN THE ROUND 75

    Beginning Your Round 75

    4 Steps to work the second round of single crochet 81

    Working in Round with Double or Treble Crochet 82

    Working in a Spiral 83

CHAPTER 9 – THE GRANNY SQUARE 86

    The Granny Square First Round 86

    Granny Square Second Round 90

    Granny Square Round Three and Beyond 93

CHAPTER 10 – GETTING GAUGE 95

    Is it Important? 95

    How Do I Get Gauge 96

    What if my Gauge Doesn´t Match? 97

CHAPTER 11 – COMMON ABBREVIATIONS AND SYMBOLS 98

    Standard Yarn Chart 102

INTRODUCTION

Crochet is easy, fun to learn, and has so many possibilities for to you to be creative that I am sure you'll want to get started right away. Using a simple crochet hook and some yarn, string, or even thread, you create loops by pulling your yarn through other loops to create your fabric. Using this simple idea of connecting loops people have made everything from fine laces to wooly warmers, like hats and scarves, and even thicker things like carpets and crocheted baskets.

Unlike other needle crafts crochet is very forgiving. If you make a mistake, you can just pull out your loops until you get back to your error, repair it, and then pick up the next loop and carry on. You can measure on the go as you crochet, simply remove your hook, hold the piece up against whatever or whoever you might be fitting, and you will soon know if you need to add or subtract stitches or make your item longer.

Crochet is also wonderfully portable. You can put a ball of yarn in your purse, or carry-all and crochet in the car, or while talking or watching TV. Some people even crochet while they walk!

Once you learn a few basic stitches, how to read a pattern and put in some practice time the doors to an amazing amount of creativity will be open to you. You will soon be able to crochet all of the lovely designs you see in magazines and online; even those funny amigurumi animals made so popular by the Japanese people. If you want to make something simple like placemats or washcloths you won't even need a pattern, just chain enough stitches for the width and keep adding rows until your item is large enough and then tie it off.

You can work with all kinds of yummy yarns in hundreds of colors and textures. But, as with every new skill, it will take a little time to become proficient at it. You will improve every time you pick up your hook and yarn. If you get stuck, refer back to this little book for help, ask your friends, or drop in at your local yarn shop. You will soon find out that crocheters are a friendly helpful bunch.

Ready to get started? Let's begin.

CHAPTER 1 – ESSENTIAL EQUIPMENT

All you need to get started with crochet is a ball of yarn and a crochet hook. Yep, it's that easy. When you are learning it is always easier to see your stitches when you work with a lighter yarn rather than a dark one. So, when choosing your yarn to stay away from colors like black or navy blue and pick a lighter hue.

The size of the crochet hook you use is directly related to the size of the yarn. If you are using a big bulky yarn, then you are going to need a large crochet hook, and at the other end of the spectrum, if you are making delicate lace you will be using a very small hook. Here is an example of a medium-sized crochet hook and what all the different areas are called.

5 AREAS OF A CROCHET HOOK

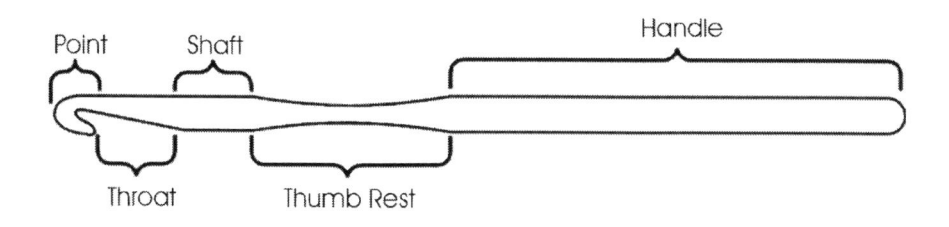

Fig. 1

POINT

The tip of the hook that is used to enter the loops of crocheted yarn.

THROAT

The throat is the little gap where the loop of yarn is held. There are two types of throats: some are tapered like the one in Figure 1, and some have an even deeper taper and a cutout cavity to hold the loop securely. This type of throat is called an in-line throat. See Figure 2.

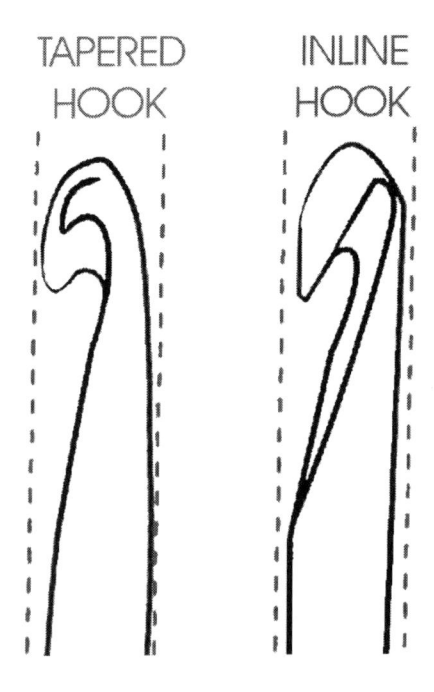

TAPERED HOOK   INLINE HOOK

Fig. 2

The tapered throat helps to hold the yarn securely and is favored by crocheters who regularly drop loops. The in-line hook is popular with crocheters who snag or split their yarn. The only way to be sure which works well for you is to try both styles.

The Shaft

This is the part of the hook just above the throat, and it can be either tapered or cylindrical. I prefer to use a tapered shaft, but some crocheters believe that a cylindrical shaft helps create even tension.

The Thumb Rest

The portion of the hook where you rest your thumb. Some thumb rests are made of a rubbery silicone substance which makes them very comfortable. Other thumb rests are made of the same material as the rest of the hook.

The Handle

The portion of the hook held by you when crocheting. The most popular style these days is the ergonomic design called the Clover Soft Touch™. This type of hook is available in almost all yarn shops and online. There are other types of crochet hooks, of course, made from steel, metal, plastic, wood and even bamboo and you can try as many as you wish.

Now that you are aware of the different features of the parts of a crochet hook you can try different types and see what works for you.

We are all unique, so what works for one crocheter may end up being unpleasant for another. Shop around, ask other crocheters if you can borrow their hooks to try them out before you make a purchase.

Other Types of Crochet Hooks

Susan Bates™ makes a line of bamboo-handled crochet hooks designed to be used for thread crochet. They have wider handles and offer a good grip while working with such a fine yarn.

Addi Swing Hooks™ have a specially designed ergonomic handle which is especially popular with those who suffer from arthritis.

The Sharp™ crochet hook has a very pointed tip, which is used to poke holes in the fabric when crocheting trim onto blankets or other fabrics.

Choosing Your Yarn

All the information you need to choose your yarn is on the yarn label. Look at the label below, and we can go through it together.

MY YARNS

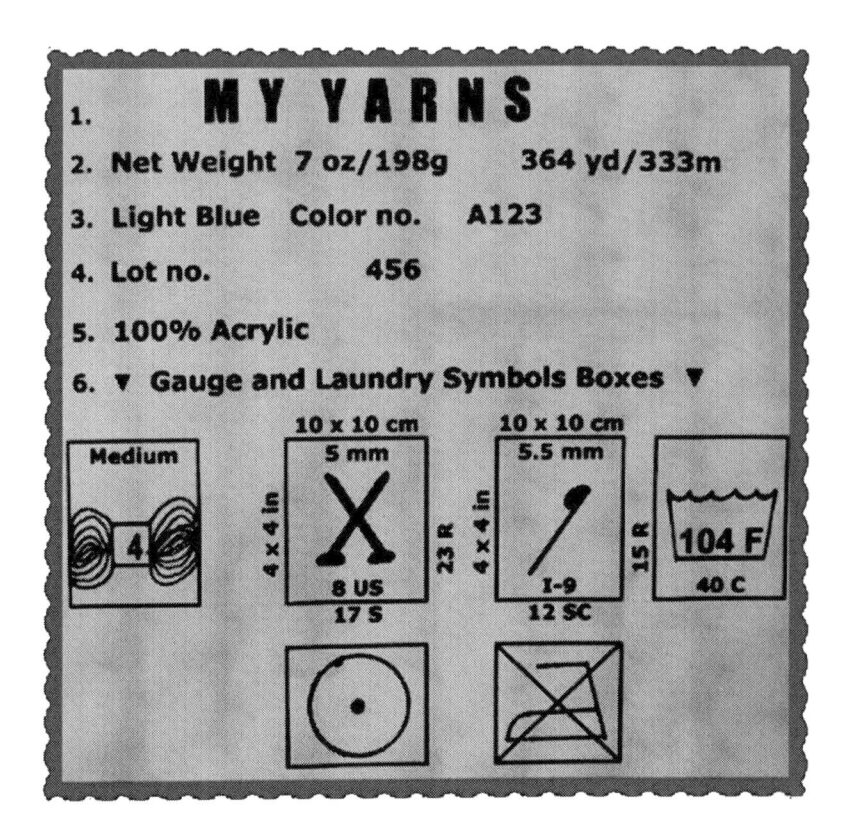

1.
2. Net Weight 7 oz/198g   364 yd/333m
3. Light Blue   Color no.   A123
4. Lot no.   456
5. 100% Acrylic
6. ▼ Gauge and Laundry Symbols Boxes ▼

Fig. 3

First, it tells you the name of the yarn company. In this case 'MY YARNS'. Then it tells you the net weight of the ball, which is 7 ounces or 198 grams. Next, it tells you that there are 364 yards or 333 meters of yarn in this ball. The yarn company calls this yarn Light Blue and gives it a color number A123 and a Lot number of 456.

Note: The Lot number is essential information for you. If you are creating something that requires more than one ball of the same colored yarn you will want the lot numbers to match, they should all be the same. Why? Because when the yarn is dyed it is done so in lots or batches and each lot can be, and probably will be, slightly different from the next.

So if you were to crochet something like an afghan that is meant to be all one shade of blue, and your color lots are different numbers you will end up with stripes of different shades of blue in your finished work. It can be very hard to see the differences with the naked eye, especially when the yarn is still on balls, so always check that your lot color numbers match.

The next item tells us what the yarn is made of. In this case, it is 100% acrylic. You need to consider what sort of yarn you will be working with. Wool and other natural fibers may need to be hand washed in cold water or even dry cleaned. If you are making something that will require a lot of laundering you may want to use a washable wool or an acrylic yarn.

The first box shows us that this is a medium type yarn, also known as a number 4. Yarn sizes are standardized these days, and at the end of this book, you will find a chart that lists them and what they mean.

The second box gives us the knitting gauge for this type of yarn. We can safely ignore this because we are learning to crochet.

The third box gives us the gauge that the maker recommends for this yarn when crocheting with it. In this case, it is telling us that the manufacturer recommends using a number 5.5 mm crochet hook, which is also known as an I or No. 9 hook. And the numbers 12 s.c. and 15 r. tell us that the yarn company expects you that using this yarn and a 5.5 mm hook you will be able to make 12 single crochet stitches every 4 inches or 10 centimeters and you will be able to crochet 15 rows of single crochet over 4 inches or 10 centimeters.

We will return to the importance of getting gauge later in Chapter 10.

The fourth box is a laundry symbol that tells us that this yarn can be washed in warm water up to 104F or 40C.

The fifth box shows a circle with a dot in the center which tells us that this yarn can be safely tumbled dry on a low setting.

The final box shows an iron with an X through it, which indicates that you should not iron any item made from this yarn.

If you are using a pattern for your crochet it will recommend, if not a particular yarn, then at least a type of yarn, perhaps chunky, or medium, or fine. A quick check of yarn labels at your local yarn sharp should give you a fair number of options to choose from.

As a beginner just learning to crochet, I recommend using a 5mm or a 5.5mm crochet hook and a medium sized yarn in a light color. By using a light color you will be able to see your stitches more easily, and by using a medium-sized hook, you won't have to struggle with stitches that are very small or very large.

The Difference between American and British Crochet Terms

American and British crochet terms differ slightly, and this can be very confusing to the beginner. The first thing you need to do is to determine if your pattern is written using the American method or the British method. Sometimes this is as easy as looking at where a magazine was published. I have created a chart below to show you the differences. The stitches are the same, but they have different names as you will see.

In this little book, we will be using the American system for crochet stitches. It is a pity that the two systems have not been merged into one, but perhaps one day they will be.

Until then if you are uncertain you can always ask at your local yarn shop, they should be able to tell you which system is being used in your pattern by looking at a photograph of the object to be crocheted or the chart being used in the pattern if there is one.

CROCHET ABBREVIATIONS

Crochet Abbreviations

Use this chart to convert UK crochet terms to US terms when needed.

UK		US	
Chain	Ch	Chain	Ch
Slip Stitch	Ss	Slip Stitch	Ss
Double Crochet	Dc	Single Crochet	Sc
Half Treble	Htr	Half Double	hdc
Treble	Tr	Double	Dc
Double Treble	dtr	Treble	Tr
Triple Treble	ttr	Double Treble	dtr

Now that we have chosen a crochet hook, some yarn, and have decided to work with the American crochet terms, we are ready to begin.

CHAPTER 2 – GETTING STARTED

4 Steps to a Slip Knot

To begin, we will make a slip knot, which is a simple knot that will snug up, or become smaller as you pull on either end of it. Here is how to make a slip knot to begin your crochet work.

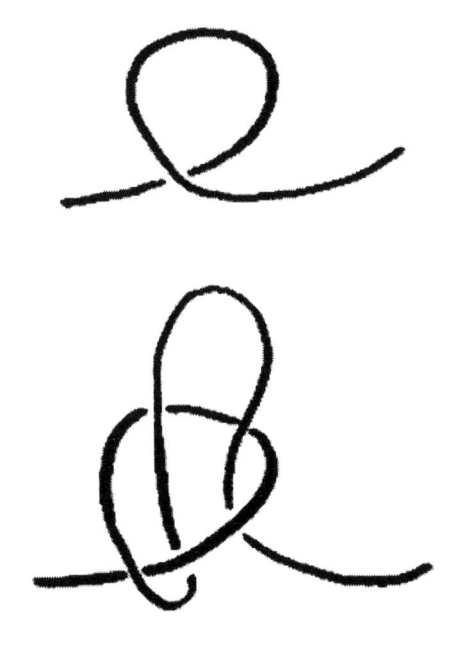

Fig. 4

1. Lay your yarn out on a flat surface as you see in the upper drawing of Figure 4, making a

loop with the yarn crossing towards the bottom.

2. The tail to the right is the free end of the yarn, and the tail to the left is the ball end of the yarn.
3. Using your fingers or your crochet hook pull some yarn through this loop using the left yarn from the ball end to create a shape as you see in the bottom of Figure 4.
4. Insert your crochet hook into this loop and pull it snug, but not tight, against the crochet hook.

Holding the Hook

There are many ways to hold your hook. I will show you the two most popular methods, and I suggest that you experiment and find what feels most comfortable for you.

The first position is similar to holding a knife. Your hand goes over the crochet hook with the handle resting against your palm and your thumb and the third finger gripping the thumb rest for movement.

The second position is like holding a pencil. Hold the hook as you would hold a pencil with your thumb and index finger on the thumb rest and the third finger near the tip of the hook. The crochet hook should be turned slightly towards you rather than facing up or down.

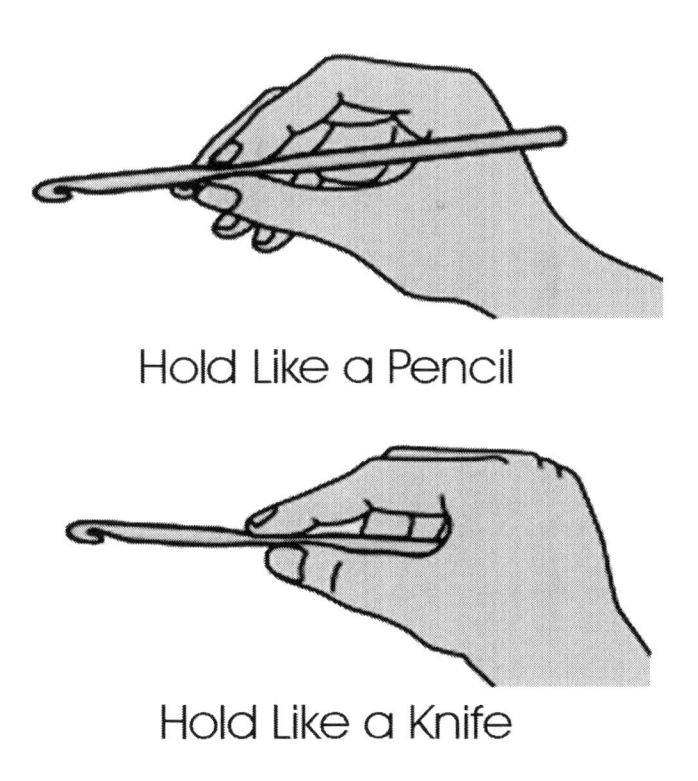

Hold Like a Pencil

Hold Like a Knife

Fig. 5

The hook should be held firmly but not tightly; this will only exhaust your hand. As a beginner you will probably grip too tightly but as you practice a little your hand will relax.

MAKING A CHAIN

The chain stitch is simply a series of loops connected to one another. They are easy to make, but you will want to practice making a few chains so that you can develop smooth stitches that are the same size, or as close to the same size as you can get. As you practice crochet, your stitches will become more uniform but as a beginner practice will help.

HERE IS HOW TO MAKE A CHAIN IN CROCHET

1. First make a slip knot, as we talked about above. Then hold the base of the slip knot with the thumb and index finger of your left hand.

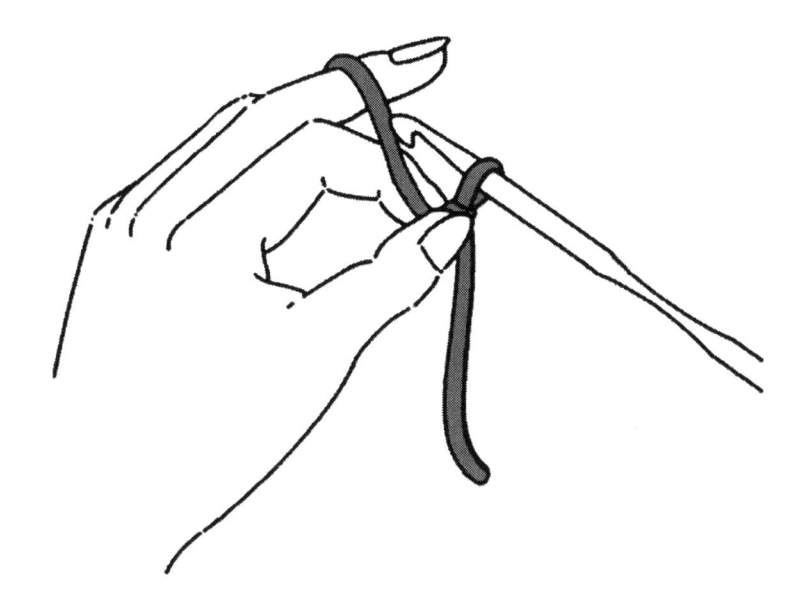

Fig. 6

2. With the yarn in your left hand, bring the yarn over the crochet hook, from back to front, and then hook the yarn through the slip knot. See Figure 7 below. You have made your first chain. See Fig. 8.

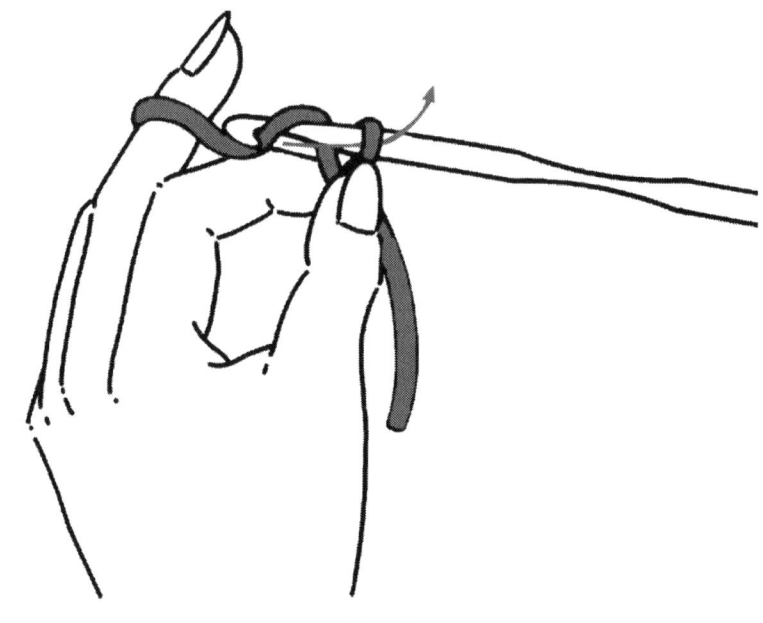

Fig. 7

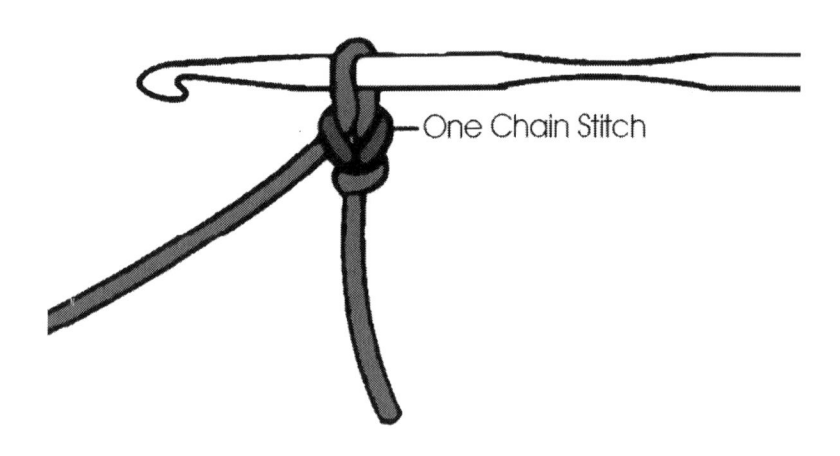

One Chain Stitch

Fig. 8

3. To continue, once again hold the base of the slip knot and bring the yarn over the crochet hook, from back

Page 24

to front, and hook it. Bring the hooked yarn through the loop on the hook. You have made another chain stitch. See Figure 9.

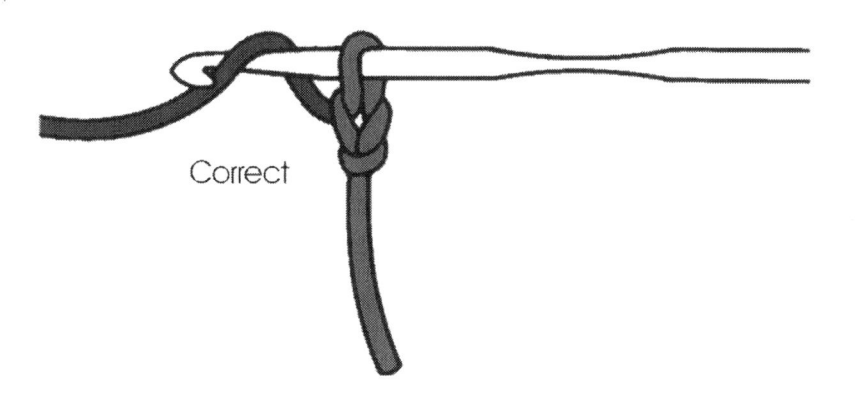

Correct

Fig. 9

4. You merely repeat this maneuver to create as many stitches as you want.

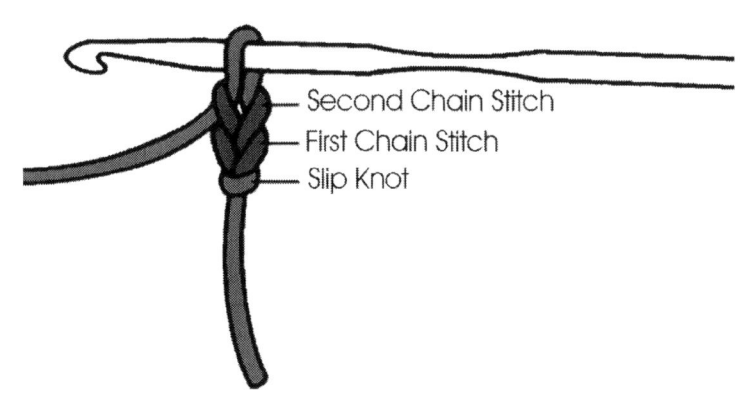

Second Chain Stitch
First Chain Stitch
Slip Knot

Fig. 10

In figure 11 below you can see that the yarn is draped over the middle finger of the left hand and possibly wrapped around the little finger. This gives the yarn some tension. You might want to try this and see if it improves your stitching.

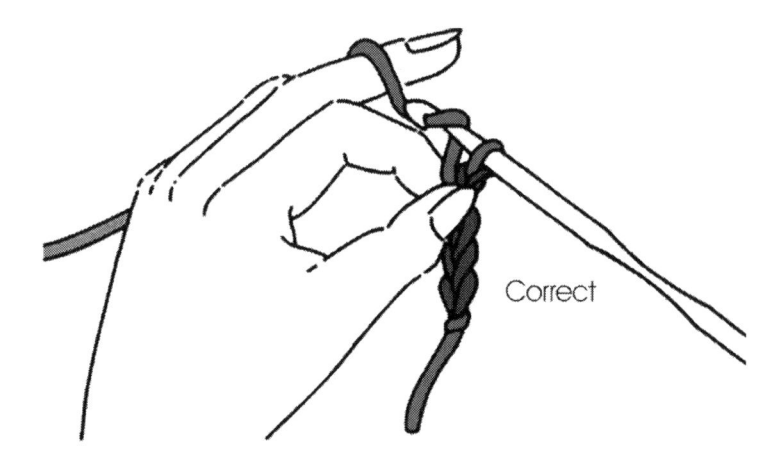

Correct

Fig. 11

Now that you know how to make a chain, your first step in crochet, I would strongly suggest that for your first practice session you do nothing but make chains of various lengths.

As you crochet your chains see if adjusting your grip on the hook or adjusting the way you hold the yarn in your left-hand makes a difference in how easily and how smoothly you can chain.

Your goal is to find a method that suits you without tiring your hands that also produces relatively even stitches. Your work will not be perfect at first, but every time you practice, it will improve.

WHICH IS THE RIGHT SIDE?

If you take a look at your chain, you will see that each stitch as a right side (the front) and a wrong side (the back). The right side of the chain is smooth, and the back side has a bump in each stitch. See Fig. 12 below.

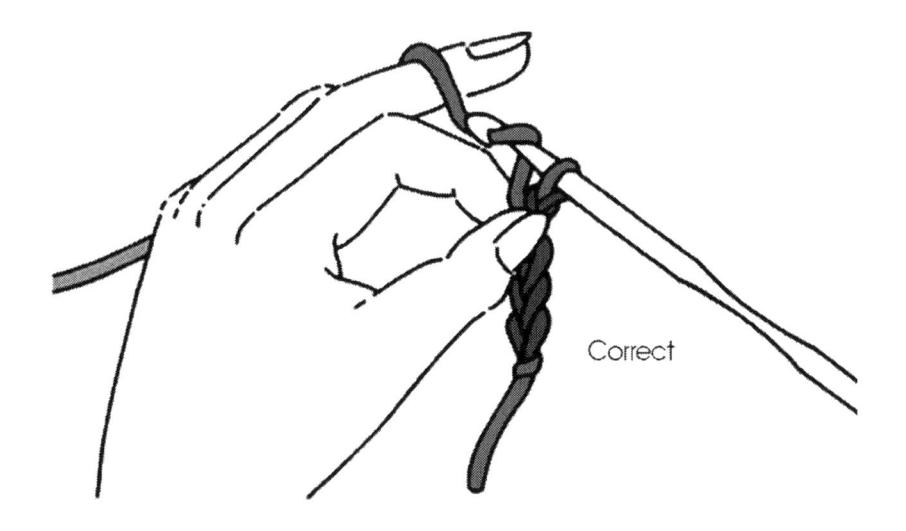

Correct

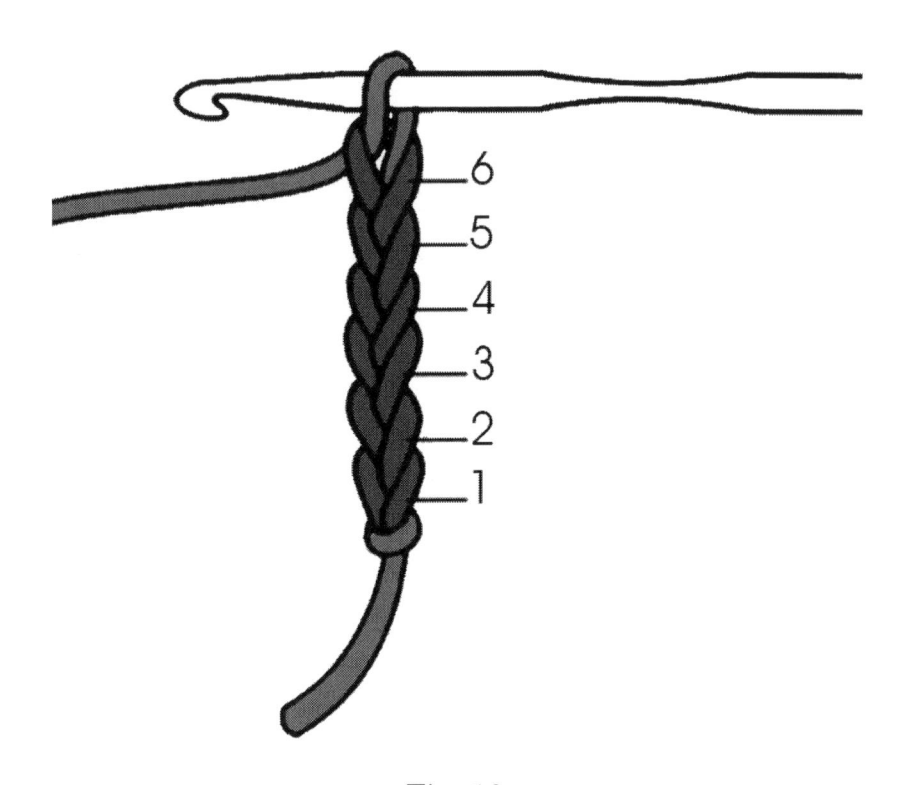

Fig. 12

The front looks like a series of interlocking V-shapes. The back has a series of bumps or bars across each stitch. See Fig. 13 below.

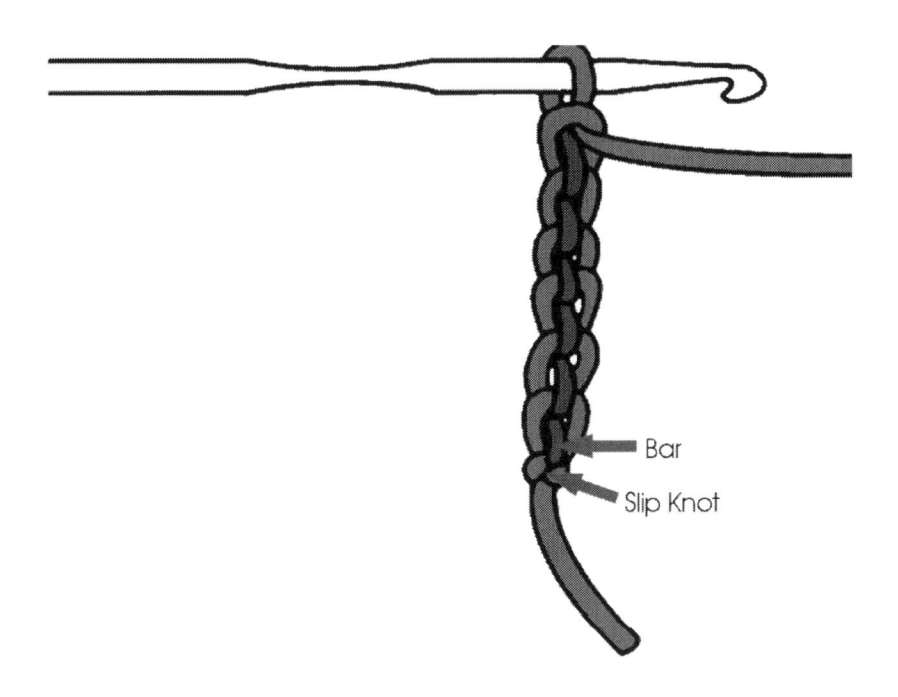

Fig. 13

CHAPTER 3 – THE SINGLE CROCHET STITCH

The single crochet is the first stitch everyone learns, and it is used in virtually all types of crochet either alone or in combination with other stitches. Below I will show you how to create the single crochet stitch (sc), and we will complete a row of single crochet.

1. Make a slip knot and chain 11 stitches. When counting your chains DO NOT COUNT the slip knot as a stitch.
2. With the right side of the chain facing you, your hook in your right hand and the yarn in your left hand, insert the hook from front to back into the second chain from the hook through the center of the V. (Note: Not the chain on your hook, not the next chain, but the one underneath that.

To some people this seems like the third chain on the hook, but we do not count the chain on the hook when counting.)

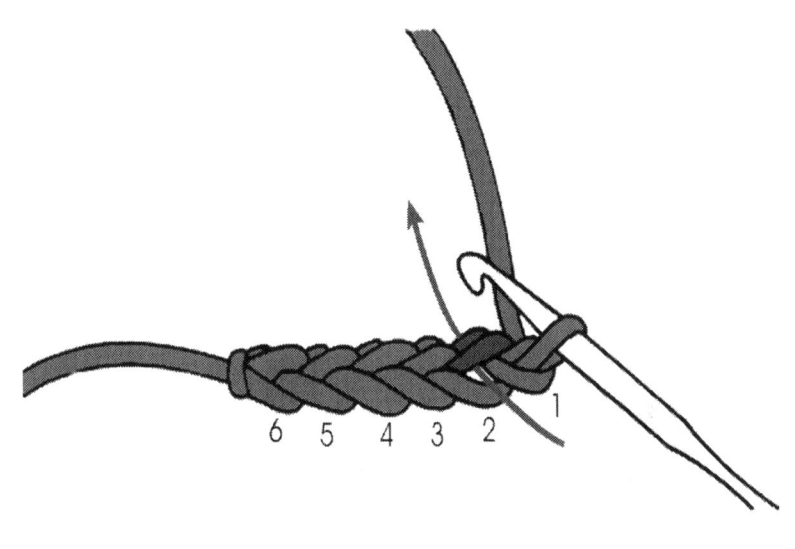

Fig. 14

3. Now, wrap the yarn over the hook from back to front.
4. Rotate the throat of the hook towards you and pull the hook through the wrapped yarn and through the stitch.

Fig. 15

5. You should now have two loops on your hook.

Fig. 16

6. Wrap the yarn over the hook again, and then rotate the throat of the hook towards you.
7. Draw the hook with the wrapped yarn through both loops on the hook. See Figure 17.

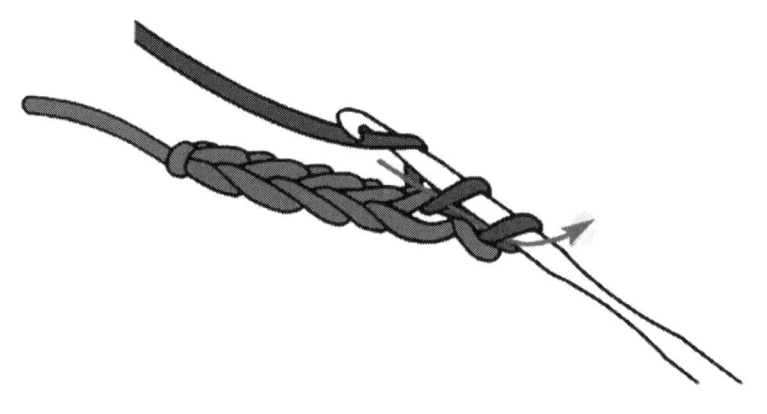

Fig. 17

8. You have completed one single crochet.

One Single Crochet

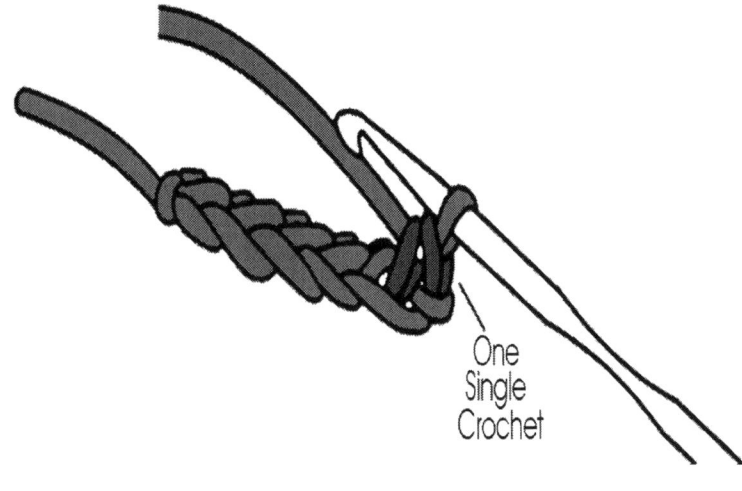

Fig. 18

Continue to single crochet across the row as follows:

1. Insert your hook from front to back into the center of the V of the next chain.

2. Repeat steps 3 through 8 above to complete your second single crochet. Repeat across the row working one single crochet into each chain across the chain.

3. Make sure you work into the last chain, but NOT the slip knot. Be careful to keep the front of the work

facing you, so that your hook goes through the center of the Vs. facing you.

At the end, you should have ten single crochet stitches. But, you chained on 11 stitches to start, what happened to the 11th stitch? Remember, you worked into the second chain from the hook, so you skipped one chain.

The skipped chain is known as a "turning chain," and it brings your yarn up to the correct level needed to work the first stitch of the next row.

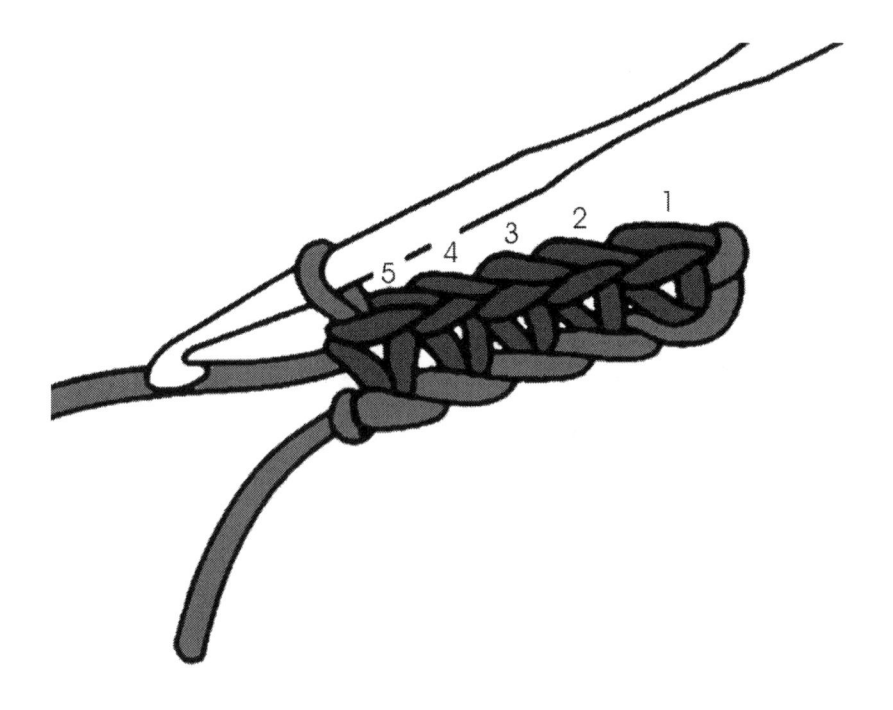

Fig. 19

Figure 20 below shows us that when working on a fabric in single crochet, we need to chain one stitch at the beginning of the row to bring the yarn up to the correct level.

You can see if we do a half-double stitch we will need to chain two stitches to bring the yarn up to the correct level and so on. If you do not chain the required stitches as the beginning of your row the edge of your crochet will not remain square but will begin to slant to the left.

Insert Book
At Beginning of
Next Row

In 1st Stitch
In 1st Stitch
In 2nd Stitch   4 - Triple Crochet
In 2nd Stitch   3 - Double Crochet
                     2 - Half Double Crochet
                     1 - Single Crochet
                     0 - Slip Stitch

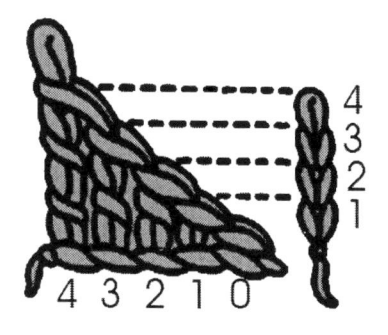

Fig. 20

Note: The turning chain almost always counts as the first stitch of the next row, <u>except when working single crochet</u>. This is because the single stitch turning chain is not wide enough to substitute for a single crochet.

WORKING THE NEXT ROW (OR TWO)

So, you have successfully crocheted a row of 10 single crochet stitches? Where do you go from here? Onward and upward.

1. Leaving your hook in the last loop, turn your work around so that you can begin a new row of single crochet.

2. Hold the completed work with your middle finger and thumb of your left hand (or whatever is most comfortable for you).

3. Make sure the working yarn coming from the ball is positioned behind your work, and the hook is held properly to make the next stitch.

Note: Each time you turn your work to crochet across the row a different side of the piece will be facing you. How do you know which is the right side? The first row of stitches, not counting your chain is normally considered the right side of the work. The easiest way to locate the right side of the work is to find the tail of the slip knot. If the tail of the slip knot is on the far right, then the right side of the work is facing you.

1. We begin the second row by making a simple chain stitch, i.e., pulling a simple loop through the loop on the hook. If you remember from figure 20 above, we require one chain stitch when working single crochet to bring the yarn up to the correct level.
2. Then we single crochet into the first stitch by inserting our hook under the top two loops of the first stitch.
3. Wrap the yarn over your crochet hook from back to front.
4. Draw the yarn through the stitch.

5. Wrap the yarn over the hook again from back to front.
6. Draw the yarn through the two loops on the hook.

You have completed one single crochet in the second row and should have one loop on your hook. To complete your row, work one single crochet into each stitch from the previous row across the work. When you get to the end count your stitches, you should have ten stitches in row two.

Making a practice square will help you learn the single crochet stitch and how to hold your hook and yarn comfortably. Also, if you make a practice square of each of the main stitches, you can compare them to note the differences. Soon you will be able to recognize the main stitches by sight, which may allow you to copy a crocheted item you see without having to purchase a pattern.

For your first square, I would recommend using some light yarn and a size I or 9 US crochet hook (5mm in the metric system).

1. Make a chain approximately four inches long. Single crochet in the second stitch from the hook and single crochet across the chain.
2. At the end of the row, turn the crochet around. Chain one to bring the yarn up to the correct height. Single crochet into the first stitch and every stitch across the row.
3. Repeat the instructions in number 2 above until you have crocheted approximately four inches.
4. Complete your last row.
5. Cut your yarn off leaving about 4 to 6 inches hanging. Wrap the yarn around your hook from back to front and pull it through the loop on the hook which will fasten off your stitching. Trim the yarn to a shorter length if desired.

CHAPTER 4 – DOUBLE CROCHET

The double crochet stitch is probably the most used stitch in crochet. You will see it is taller than the single crochet. It is made in almost the same manner; we just add a few steps.

Before we start just a little recap. Remember you never work in the first chain from the crochet hook (unless specifically told to do so in a pattern). Put your hook through the center of the V on the chain and under the bar at the back of the stitch. Do not twist the chain.

DOUBLE CROCHET ROW ONE

1. To begin our first row of double crochet, chain 20 stitches. Bring the yarn over the hook from back to front. Skip the first three chains from the hook. (Remember do not count the chain on your hook.) Insert the hook in the fourth chain.

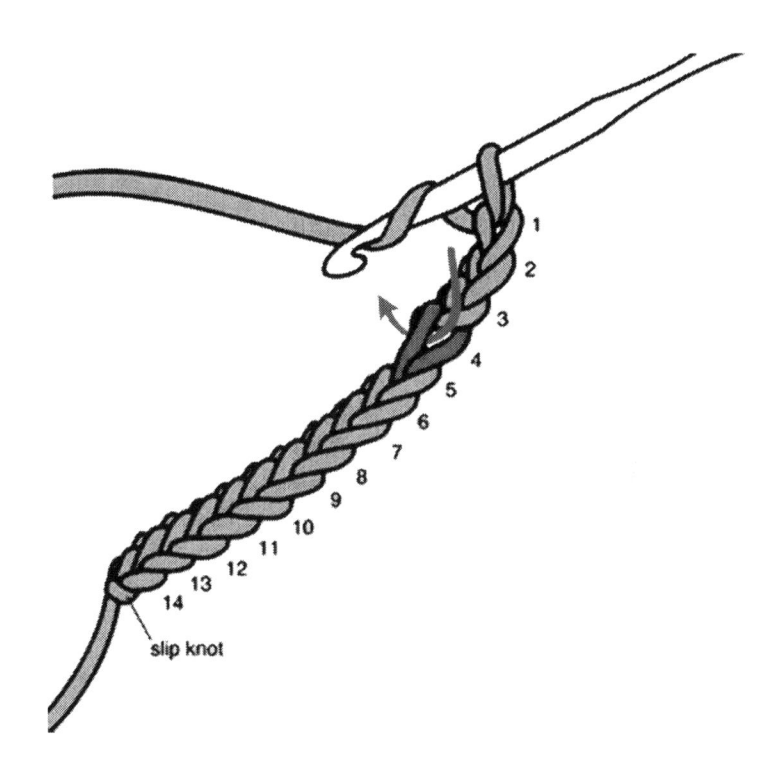

Fig 21.

2. Bring the yarn over the crochet hook from back to front and pull it through the chain stitch and up onto the shaft of the hook.

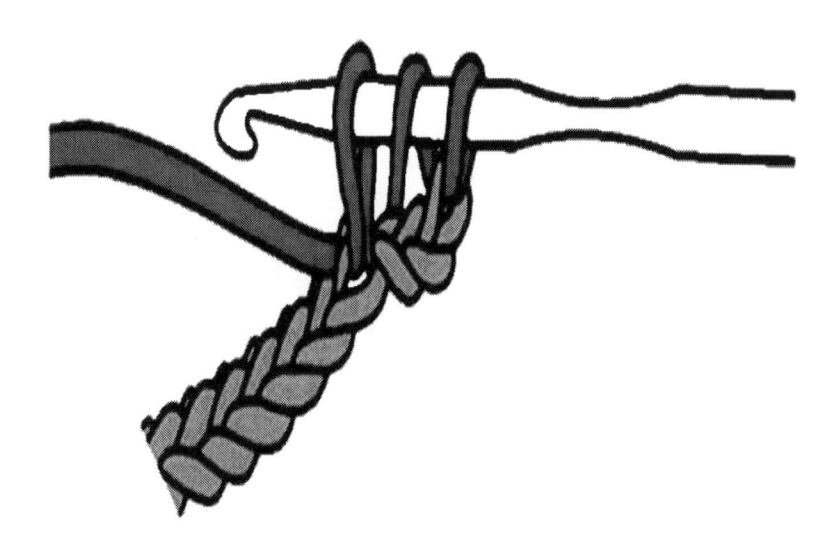

Fig. 22

3. Now bring the yarn over the crochet hook from back to front and pull the yarn through the first two loops on the hook. You will have two loops on your hook.

See figures 23 and 24 below.

Fig. 23

Fig. 24

4. Once again bring the yarn over the hook from back to front and pull through both loops on the hook.

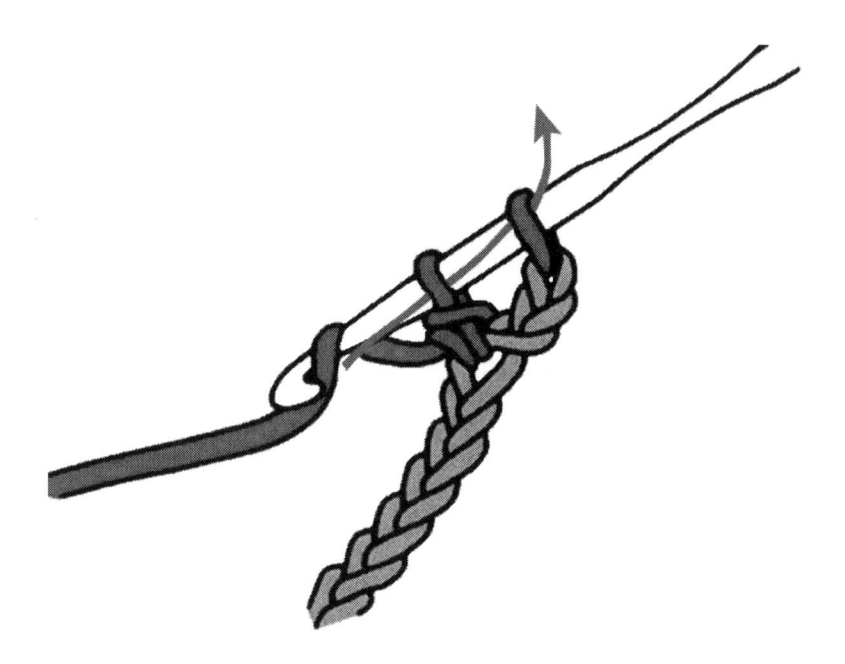

Fig. 25

5. One loop remains on the hook. You have completed your first double crochet. Notice how it is taller than the single crochet stitches you made earlier.

6. Now, continue along the row making a double crochet stitch in each chain.

7. You had 20 stitches, to begin with; then you skipped the first three chain stitches to bring your yarn up to the proper level for double crochet. Those chains formed your first stitch. So you should have 18

double crochet stitches and a single loop on your hook.

To work the next row of double crochet, you will need to chain three stitches to bring the yarn up to the correct height. These three chains also count as your first double crochet stitch in this row.

This means that you should skip the first double crochet of the row below, which is found directly at the base of your three chains stitches, and make your first double crochet stitch into the second double crochet stitch of the row below. Here is how to complete your second row in double crochet.

1. Chain three. Then, skip the first double crochet stitch in the row below.
2. Work a double crochet stitch in the next double crochet of the row below. Be careful to put your hook beneath both top loops of the stitch.
3. Continue making double crochet stitches in each stitch across the row.

4. Your last stitch in this row will be worked into the top of the three skipped chains from the row below. Work into the center of the V, of the top chain. See figure 26.

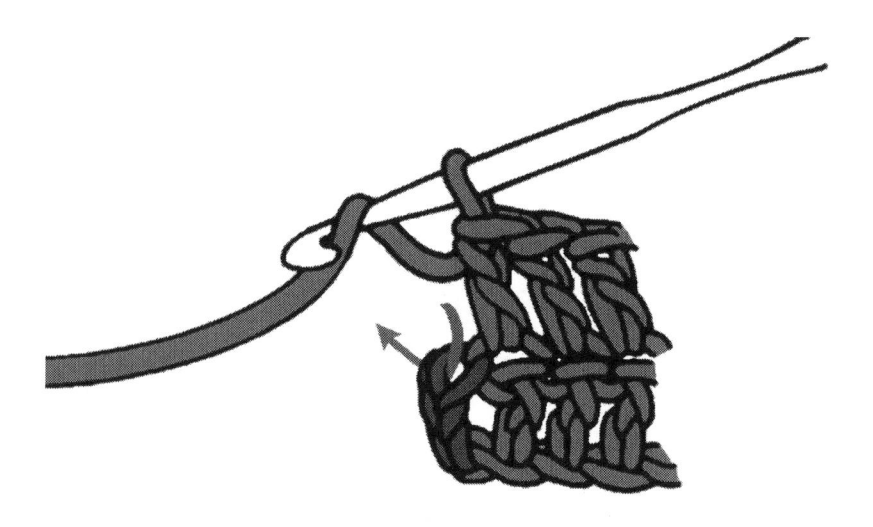

Fig. 26

Stop and count your stitches across the row. You should have 12 stitches.

For your second practice square, I would recommend using some light yarn and a size I or 9 US crochet hook (5mm in the metric system).

1. Make a chain approximately four inches long. Double crochet into the fourth stitch from the hook and double crochet across the chain.
2. At the end of the row, turn the crochet around. Chain three to bring the yarn up to the correct height. Double crochet into the first stitch and every stitch across the row.
3. Repeat the instructions in number 2 above until you have crocheted approximately four inches.
4. Complete your last row.
5. Cut your yarn off leaving about 4 to 6 inches hanging. Wrap the yarn around your hook from back to front and pull it through the loop on the hook which will fasten off your stitching. Trim the yarn to a shorter length if desired.

CHAPTER 5 – TREBLE CROCHET

The treble crochet stitch is even longer than the double crochet stitch but as you may have guessed, it is made in the same way, but we just have to pull through more loops one extra time.

To bring the yarn up to the required height for this stitch we will need to chain four for the turning chain, and in the first row, we will need to put our hook into the fifth chain from the hook.

7 STEPS TO MAKE YOUR FIRST ROW OF TREBLE CROCHET

1. Make a slip knot and chain 25 stitches.

2. Wrap the yarn around the crochet hook, from back to front, **twice**.

3. Skip the first four chains and then insert the hook into the fifth chain from the hook.

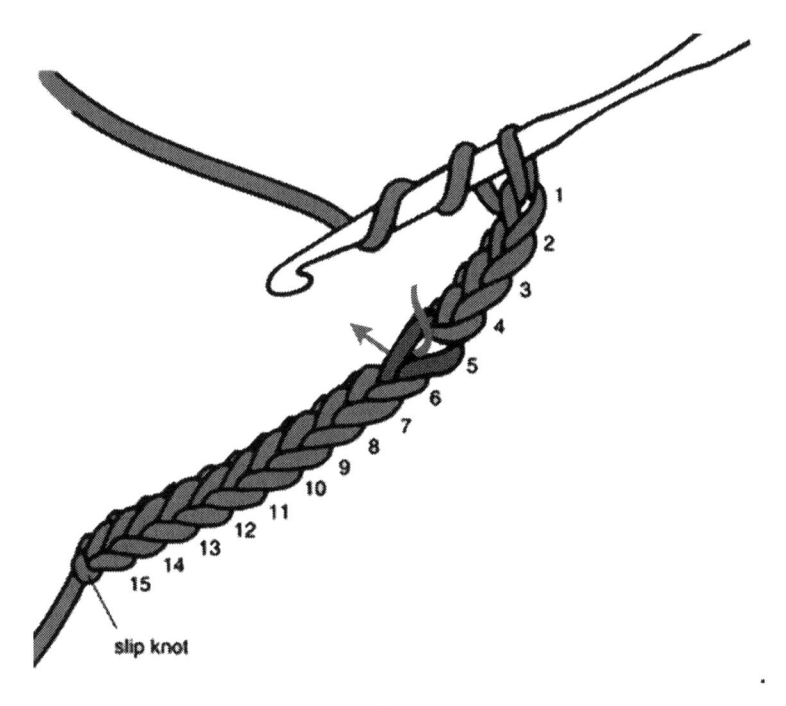

Fig. 27

4. Bring the yarn over the hook, from back to front, and pull the yarn through the chain stitch and up to the throat of your hook. You now have four loops on your hook.

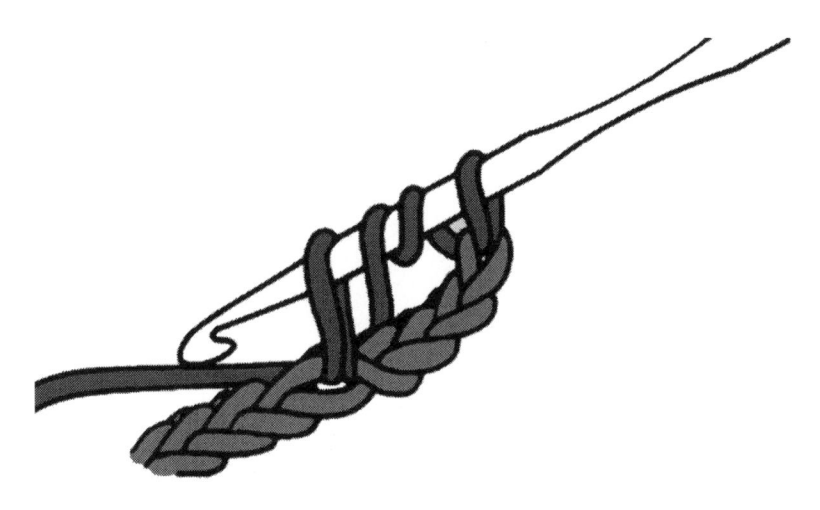

Fig. 28

5. Bring the yarn over the crochet hook and pull it through the first two loops on the hook. You now have three loops on the hook.

Fig. 29

Fig. 30

6. Bring the yarn over the crochet hook and pull it through the next two loops on the hook. You have two loops on the hook.

Fig. 31

Fig. 32

7. Bring the yarn over the crochet hook and pull the yarn through the last two loops on the hook.

Fig 33

You have completed one treble crochet.

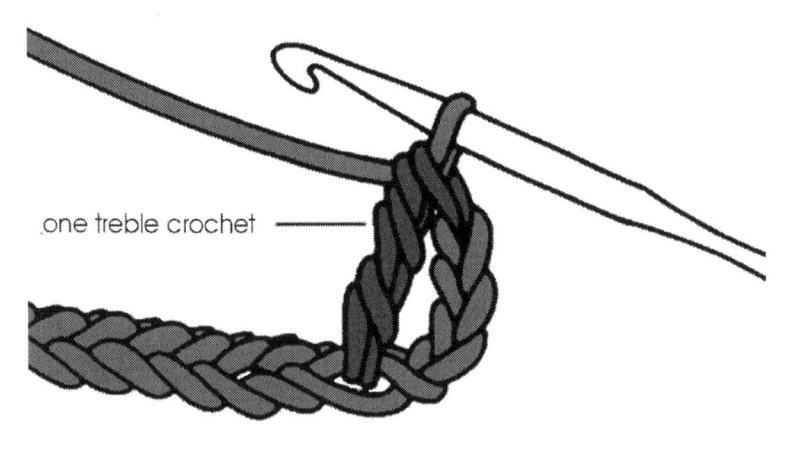

Fig 34

For your third practice square, I would recommend using some light yarn and a size I or 9 US crochet hook (5mm in the metric system).

1. Make a chain approximately four inches long. Treble crochet into the fourth stitch from the hook and treble crochet across the chain.

2. At the end of the row, turn the crochet around. Chain four to bring the yarn up to the correct height. Treble crochet into the first stitch and every stitch across the row.

3. Repeat the instructions in number 2 above until you have crocheted approximately four inches.

4. Complete your last row.

5. Cut your yarn off leaving about 4 to 6 inches hanging. Wrap the yarn around your hook from back to front and pull it through the loop on the hook which will fasten off your stitching. Trim the yarn to a shorter length if desired.

CHAPTER 5 – HALF DOUBLE CROCHET

The half double crochet stitch is a strange little stitch. It is made the same way the other stitches are, but it is the only stitch that is made with three loops instead of two or groups of two.

HERE IS HOW TO MAKE THE HALF DOUBLE CROCHET STITCH

Make a slip knot and chain 13. Bring the yarn over the crochet hook, from back to front. Skip the first two chains and insert the hook into the third chain from the hook.

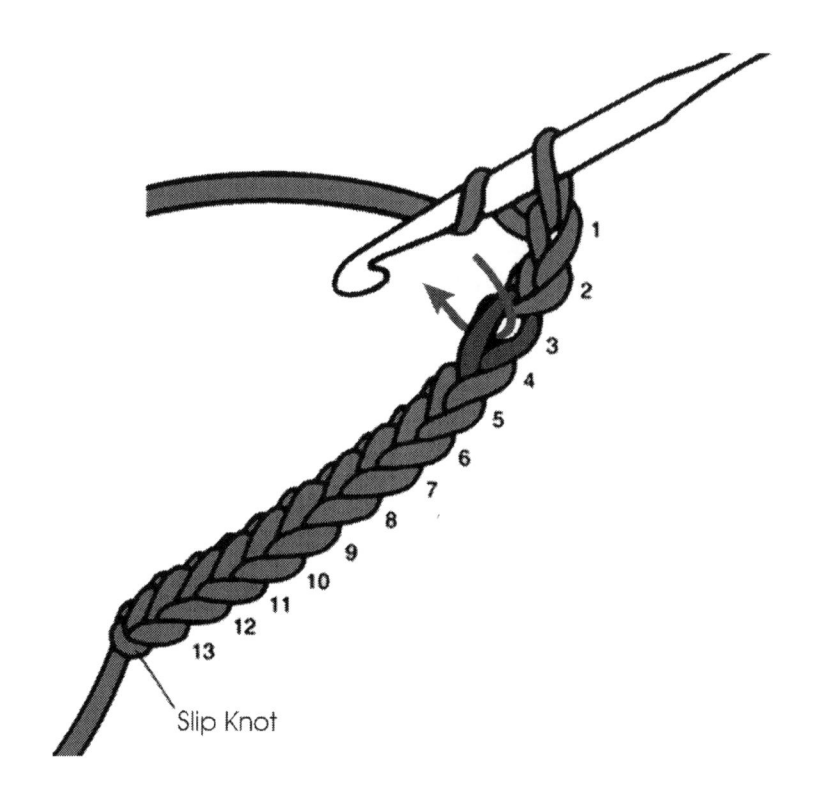

Fig. 35

Bring the yarn over the crochet hook, from back to front, and pull it through the chain stitch up to the throat of the crochet hook. Three loops on the hook.

Fig. 36

Bring the yarn over the crochet hook, from back to front, and pull it through all three loops on the hook.

Fig. 37

One half double crochet made.

One Half Double Crochet

Fig. 38

To complete the row, work one half double crochet in each chain across the row. Once the row is complete stop and count the stitches. You have a total of 12 half double crochets, including the first two chains you skipped at the beginning of the row, which count as a half double crochet in this case.

For your fourth practice square, I would recommend using some light yarn and a size I or 9 US crochet hook (5mm in the metric system).

1. Make a chain approximately four inches long. Half double crochet into the third stitch from the hook and half double crochet across the chain.
2. At the end of the row, turn the crochet around. Chain two to bring the yarn up to the correct height. Half double crochet in the first stitch and every stitch across the row.
3. Repeat the instructions in number 2 just above until you have crocheted approximately four inches.
4. Complete your last row.
5. Cut your yarn off leaving about 4 to 6 inches hanging. Wrap the yarn around your hook from back to front and pull it through the loop on the hook which will fasten off your stitching. Trim the yarn to a shorter length if desired.

CHAPTER 6 – INCREASING AND DECREASING

When you need to make your crochet wider you use increases. Decreases, of course, make the crochet piece narrower. Your pattern will indicate when increases or decreases are needed. The following indicates how you increase in all the stitches we have covered so far:

To practice your increases, make a practice sample as follows. Make a slip knot and chain 15 stitches. Work five rows of single crochet with 14 stitches in each row. We are going to use this sample to create increases. To increase one stitch whether, in single crochet, double crochet or treble crochet, you simply work two stitches into one stitch below.

4 STEPS TO INCREASING IN SINGLE CROCHET

1. You have made your sample single crochet fabric above.
2. Turn your work and chain one.
3. Single crochet in the first two stitches.

4. In the third stitch single crochet. Once that stitch is completed, put your hook back into the third stitch and single crochet again. You now have two single crochets in one stitch, and you have made an increase.

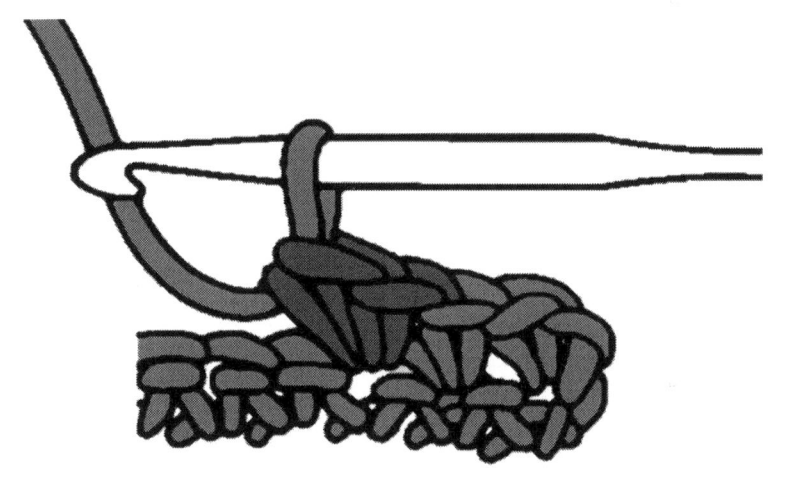

Single Crochet Increase

Fig. 39

5 STEPS TO DOUBLE CROCHET INCREASE

To make a double crochet increase you simple work a second double crochet stitch into a particular stitch below. For example,

1. Make a slip knot and chain 15 stitches.

2. Work five rows of double crochet with 13 stitches in each row.

3. Turn your work and double crochet two stitches.

4. In the third stitch double crochet once and when that stitch is complete put your hook into the same stitch and double crochet a second time.

5. One double crochet increase completed.

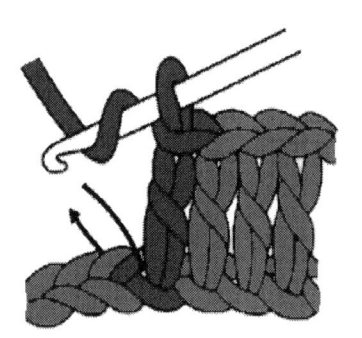

Fig. 40

INCREASING IN TREBLE CROCHET

1. Read how to increase in single crochet above.
2. You do the same thing, except you will treble crochet twice into the same stitch below.

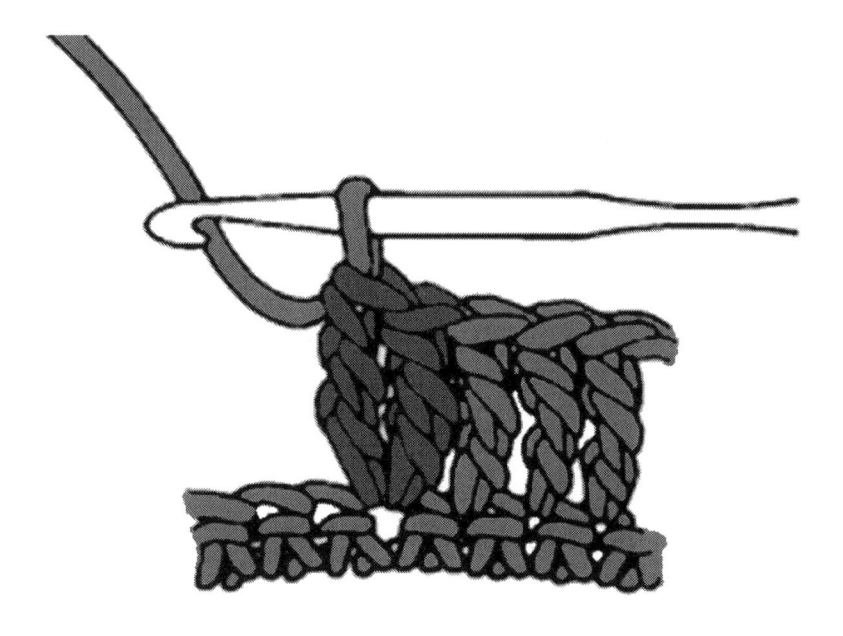

Fig. 41

INCREASING IN HALF DOUBLE CROCHET

1. Read how to increase in single crochet above.
2. You do the same thing, except you will half double crochet twice into the same stitch below.

Half Double Crochet Increase

Fig. 42

4 Steps to Decreasing in Single Crochet

1. To decrease a stitch in single crochet, you simply insert your hook into the next stitch and pull up a loop.

2. You have two loops on your hook.

3. Now, insert your hook into the next stitch and pull up a loop there as well. You have three loops on your hook.

4. Wrap the yarn around your hook, from back to front, and pull it through all three loops on the hook. You have decreased your crochet fabric by one stitch in width.

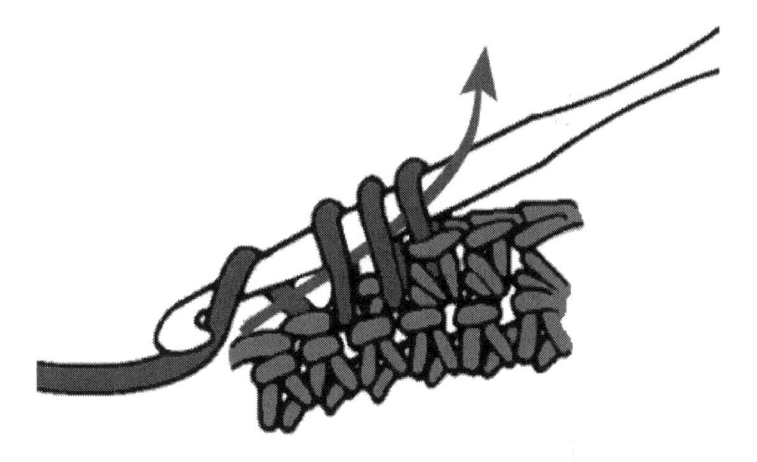

Fig. 43

4 Steps to Decreasing in Double Crochet

1. To decrease a stitch in double crochet first work a double crochet in the stitch until two loops are left on your hook.

Fig. 44

2. Keep these two loops on the hook.
3. Work another double crochet in the next stitch until three loops remain on the hook.
4.

Fig 45

5. Hook the yarn, from back to front, and pull it through all three loops on the hook. One double crochet decrease made.

Fig. 46

12 STEPS TO DECREASING IN TREBLE CROCHET

<u>To decrease a stitch in treble crochet:</u>

1. Yarn around hook twice.

2. Insert hook in the indicated stitch.

3. Yarn around hook, pull up a loop.

4. Yarn around hook, pull yarn through two loops on hook.
5. Yarn around hook, pull yarn through two loops on hook.
6. Yarn around hook twice.
7. Insert hook in the indicated stitch.
8. Yarn around hook, pull up a loop.
9. Yarn around hook, pull yarn through two loops on hook.
10. Yarn around hook, pull yarn through two loops on hook.
11. You now have three loops on your hook.

Fig. 47

12. Yarn around hook and pull it through all three loops to complete your decrease.

6 STEPS TO HALF DOUBLE CROCHET DECREASE

1. To decrease a stitch on half double crochet:

2. Yarn around the hook.

3. Insert hook in next stitch and draw up a loop. Three loops on hook.

Fig. 48

4. Yarn over hook.

5. Keeping these three loops on the hook, yarn around hook and pull up a loop into the next stitch.

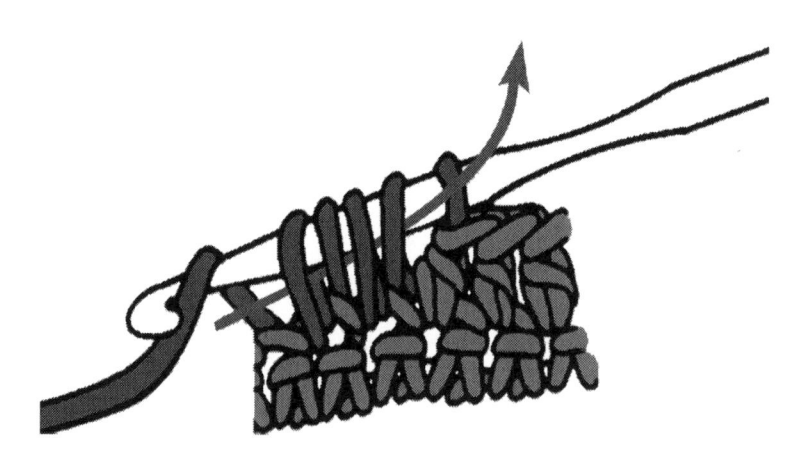

Fig. 49

6. One half double crochet decrease made.

Fig. 50

CHAPTER 7 – CHANGING COLORS AS YOU CROCHET

Changing colors in crochet is easy. If you are making stripes, you just add the new color with the first stitch you chain on a new row.

If you want to change colors in the middle of a row, you work the last stitch in the old color, up until the point you pull the last loop through the loops on the hook. This is the step-by-step process.

CHANGING COLORS IN SINGLE CROCHET

I am going to assume you have made a chain and used single crochet to make the first row. In the second row, you single crochet a few stitches until your pattern indicates to change colors in two stitches.

1. For the last stitch in the old color, insert your hook from front to back into the center V of the next chain or stitch.
2. Wrap the yarn around the hook and pull the stitch through and onto your hook. You should now have two loops of the old color on your hook.

3. Using the new color, wrap it around your hook, and pull it through the two loops on your hook.

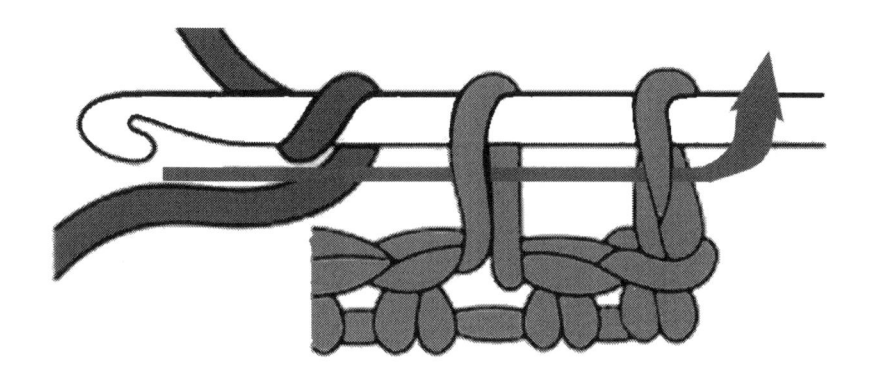

Fig. 51

CHANGING COLORS IN DOUBLE CROCHET

The method is the same in the double crochet stitches.

1. Complete the last stitch you want in the old color right up until you have the last two loops on the hook.

2. Now, add in the new color, wrap your new color around the hook and pull it through both loops completely the double crochet.

3. The new color has been started, and the double crochet in the old color has been completed.

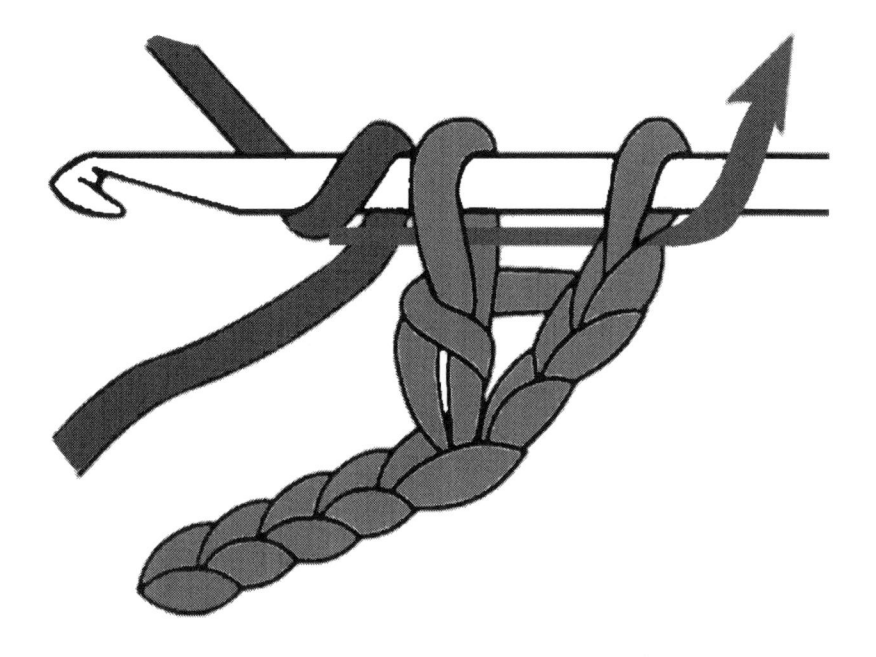

Fig. 52

CHAPTER 8 – WORKING IN THE ROUND

If you want to crochet a hat or a purse you or even a drink coaster you will need to know how to crochet in the round. This chapter will discuss the different ways to work crochet in the round.

We will use the single crochet as our example to get started. Many patterns begin working in the round with single crochet.

BEGINNING YOUR ROUND

To begin crochet in the round, you must begin with a center ring. This ring is the foundation, and all of your stitches radiate out from it. There are some different methods to do this. We will begin with working your chain stitches into a ring.

1. Make a slip knot on your hook.
2. Chain six stitches.

3. Slip stitch the chain together. Put your hook through the first stitch in your chain (not the slip knot). Yarn over hook and pull the yarn through.
4. You have now joined the chain into a ring.

Fig. 53

The number of stitches in your chain determines the size of the hole that the center ring creates, and also how many stitches you can work into that center ring. The pattern you are working on should indicate how many stitches to make in your chain, but you can adjust it larger to smaller if you find the hole is too big or too small.

You are ready to crochet your first circular round, but first, you need to determine the number of turning chains you will need.

Remember: we must always bring our yarn up to the correct level for the next row of stitches. In this case, we are using single crochet, so we know that we will require one turning chain.

1. Chain one. This is your turning chain for single crochet.
2. Insert your hook through the center of the ring.

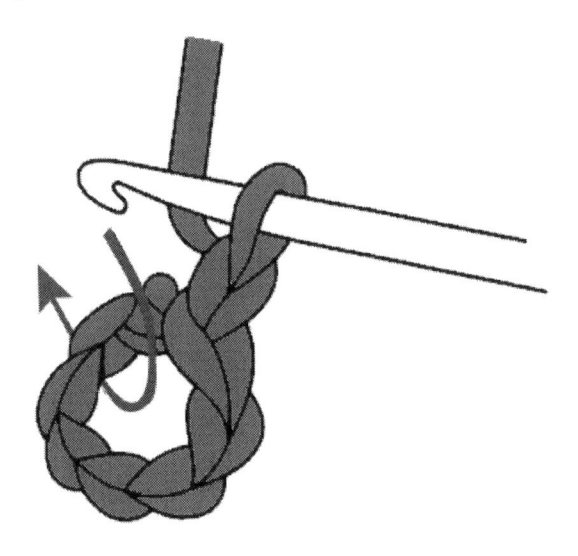

Fig. 54

3. Yarn over your hook.

4. Pull the yarn through the center ring to so you now have two loops on your hook.

5. Yarn over the hook.

6. Pull the yarn through the two loops on your hook.

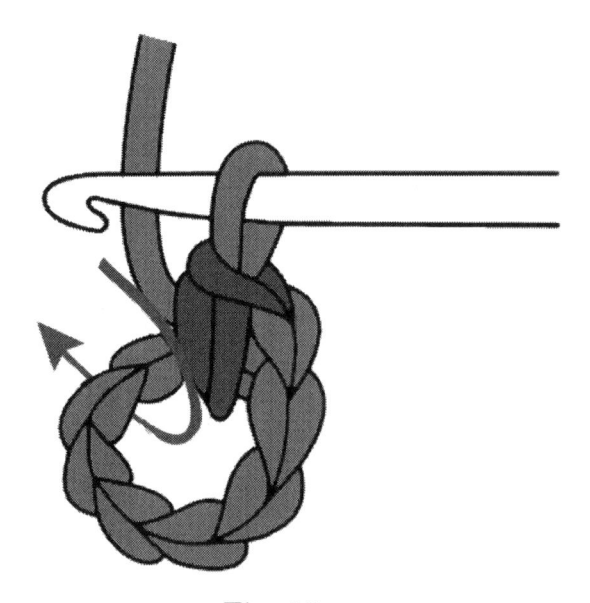

Fig. 55

You have completed your first single crochet into the ring. Continue to work single crochet stitches into the ring until you have completed ten, including your chain one.

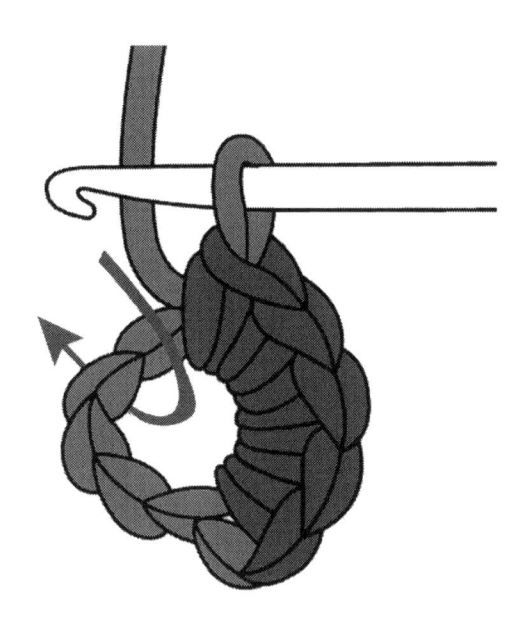

Fig 56

To join your round of single crochet stitches into a ring ready for a second round of stitches, this is what to do:

1. Skip the chain one turning chain you made and insert your hook under the top two loops of the first single crochet stitch you made.

2. Yarn over the hook.

3. Draw the yarn through the stitch and the loop on your hook. This completes one slip stitch and joins your stitches into a round.

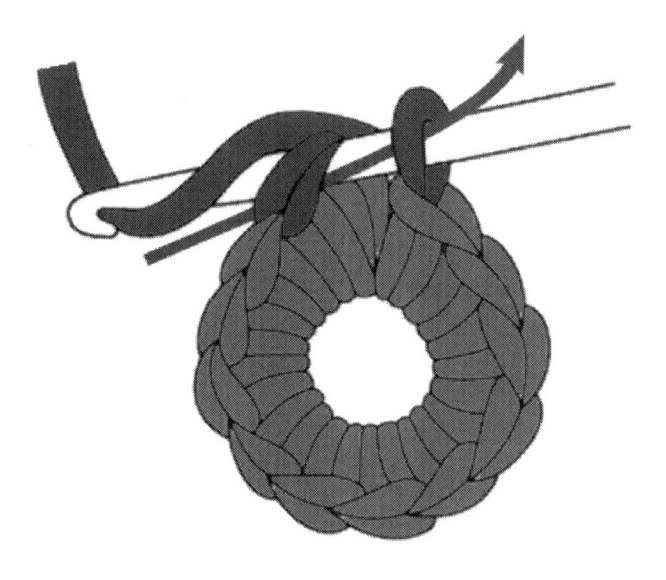

Fig. 57

You are now ready to begin adding rounds to your first row of circular crochet. It is similar to adding rows except you do not turn your work, you go around and around. Also, you need to increase the number of stitches you work in every round.

Otherwise, your crochet work will not lie flat but become a sort of thimble shape. The pattern you are working with will tell you how often to increase. You will make more increases using double and treble crochet because those stitches are long they increase the circumference of a circle more quickly than single crochet.

Page 80

4 STEPS TO WORK THE SECOND ROUND OF SINGLE CROCHET

1. After joining your first round, chain one stitch for the turning chain.
2. Do not turn your work. Work two single crochet stitches under the top two loops of the first stitch. (This is the same stitch you worked your slip stitch into.)
3. Work two single crochet stitches in each stitch all the way around the circle. You are increasing all the way around; your stitch count will double.
4. Slip stitch the first and last stitch of the round together.

Now make a practice circle of single crochet for your sample collection. Remember you will need to increase stitches every round to keep your work flat. You can experiment with increasing every stitch, or you could increase on every other stitch or every third stitch.

If you have trouble seeing the first stitch at the beginning of a row, simply put a safety pin or a crochet marker through that stitch, so you will know when you have come around to it and complete your circle with a slip stitch.

WORKING IN ROUND WITH DOUBLE OR TREBLE CROCHET

When working in the round with double crochet or any stitch other than single crochet:

1. Chain the beginning of the round. (In our example you chain ten stitches.)

2. Join those stitches into a circle by using a slip stitch, as illustrated above in the single crochet instructions.

3. Single crochet around the circle, creating as many stitches as your pattern calls for.

4. When you get to the end of the round slip stitch into the top of the starting chain. Round one is complete.

5. Now chain 3 to bring the yarn up to the correct level to begin your double crochet round.

6. For round two you are going to double crochet twice into each single crochet stitch of the previous round. This will double the number of stitches in your round, and it will lie flat.

7. Once you have completed your first row of double crochet stitches, slip stitch into the top of the turning chain to complete the round.

WORKING IN A SPIRAL

If you crochet in a circle but do not end the round with a slip stitch what happens is that you create a rounded spiral shape. Spirals are often used for simple things like coasters, or the bottom of a crocheted basket. Here is how to create a continuously growing spiral.

1. Chain the beginning of the round. (In our example you chain 8 stitches.)

2. Join those stitches into a circle by using a slip stitch, as illustrated above in the single crochet instructions.
3. Round 1- chain 1, nine single crochet into the ring.
4. Round 2 – Make two single crochet into every stitch on this round. Total of 18 stitches.
5. Round 3 – Make two single crochet into the next stitch, single crochet in the next stitch. Repeat this nine times. Total of 27 stitches.
6. Round 4 – Make two single crochet into the next stitch, single crochet into the following two stitches. Repeat this nine times. Total of 36 stitches.
7. Round 5 – Make two single crochet in the next stitch, single crochet in the next three stitches. Repeat this nine times. Total of 45 stitches.
8. Round 6 - Make two single crochet in the next stitch, single crochet in the next four stitches. Repeat this nine times. Total of 54 stitches.

You will notice that in the spiral we have created nine increases of (single crochet twice into the same stitch) in each round. And each round has one more single crochet between increases than the previous round. You can keep going with this established pattern to make a spiral as large as you wish.

CHAPTER 9 – THE GRANNY SQUARE

The granny square, so named because almost everyone's granny crocheted an afghan made of these simple motifs at one time or another.

Motifs are merely little building blocks of crochet. They can be used on their own as jewelry, coasters, doilies, or even as part of a garment. When they are put together, they can make any sort of fabric from a scarf to a giant wooly afghan to snuggle under on rainy days.

There must be thousands of different motif patterns in books and magazines. Almost all of them begin with a simple chained circle and move outward from there round by round. Below are the instructions for the most basic granny square to get you started on your journey exploring motifs. You can work the entire motif in a single color, or you can change colors for every round of the motif, the options are unlimited.

THE GRANNY SQUARE FIRST ROUND

1. Chain 4.
2. Slip stitch into the first chain to form a ring.

3. Chain 3 (This counts as your first double crochet).

4. Work two more double crochet stitches into the ring.

5. Chain 2. (This creates your first corner.)

6. Work 3 more double crochet into the ring.

7. Chain 2. (This is your second corner.)

8. Work 3 more double crochet into the ring.

9. Chain 2 (This is your third corner.)

10. Work 3 more double crochet into the ring.

11. Chain 2. (This is your fourth corner.)

12. Join the round by making a slip stitch in the top of the turning chain you began with.

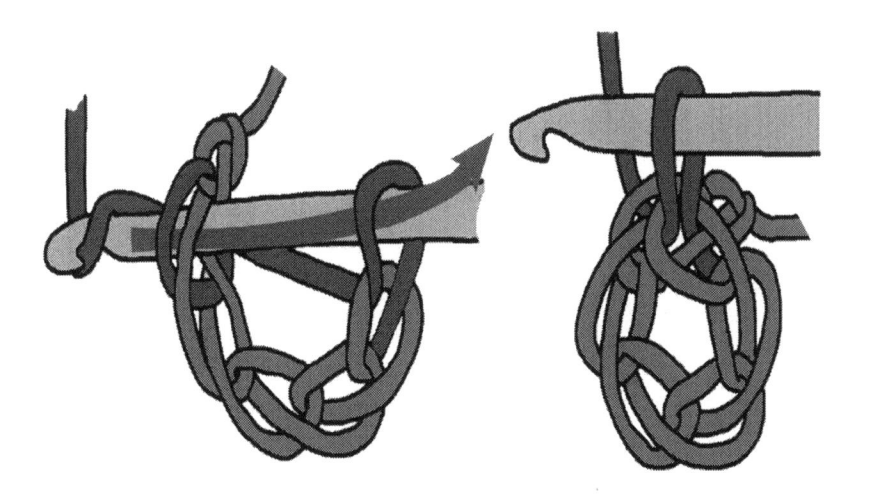

Fig. 58

Fig. 59

Fig. 60

Fig. 61

Fig. 62

GRANNY SQUARE SECOND ROUND

1. Chain 4. This brings your yarn up to the correct level. This will count as your last double crochet at the end of this round.
2. Insert your crochet hook into the first chain space to the left and make three double crochet in this space.
3. Chain three. This is your first corner of this round.

4. Insert your crochet hook back into the same first chain space and make three more double crochet.
5. Chain three. Insert your crochet hook into the second chain space of this round and make three double crochet.
6. Chain three. This is the second corner of this round.
7. Continue in this manner until you get to the last three double crochet stitches. Instead only crochet two double crochet stitches. The chain you began the round with will count as the last double crochet of this round.
8. Slip one stitch in turning chain to join.

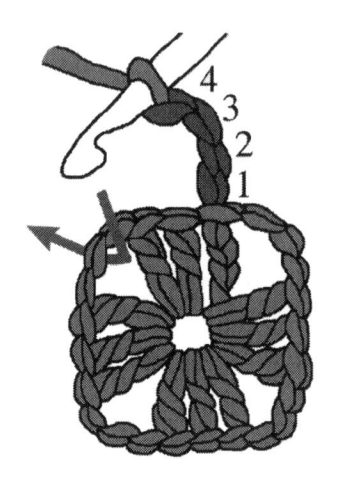

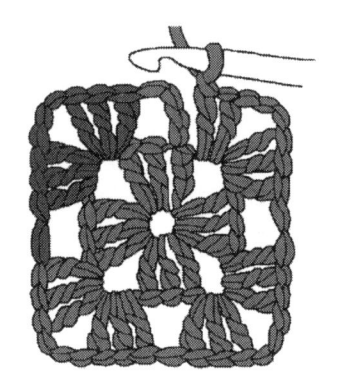

Fig. 63

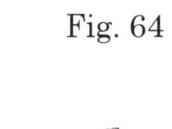

Fig. 64

Fig. 65

Fig. 66

GRANNY SQUARE ROUND THREE AND BEYOND

1. Chain 3. This brings your yarn up to the correct level.
2. Insert your crochet hook into the chain space to the left and make two double crochet in this space.

Fig. 67

3. Chain three.
4. Insert your crochet hook back into the next chain space and make three more double crochet.
5. Chain 3. This is your first corner for this round.
6. Insert your crochet hook into the same chain space and make three double crochet.

7. Chain 3.

8. Continue in this manner until you get to the last three double crochet stitches.

9. Slip one stitch in turning chain to join.

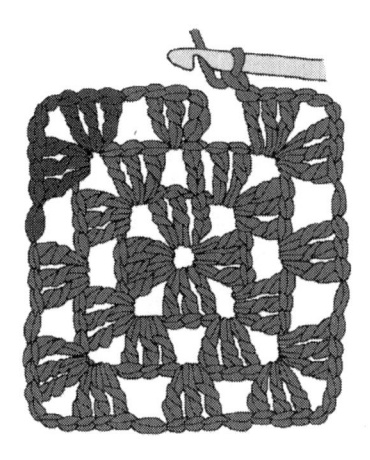

Fig. 68

CHAPTER 10 – GETTING GAUGE

What is gauge? It is the ratio of a certain number of stitches or rows to a certain number of inches. You use this ratio, which is given to you at the beginning of every pattern, to make sure your stitches are consistent and therefore the size of the item you are making will match the measurements given in the pattern.

Is it Important?

If your gauge is off by even a little bit, say one stitch to the inch, you could end up making a sweater that will fit your overweight Uncle Charlie, instead of you. Here is an example:

Let us assume you are making a sweater and the gauge called for in the pattern is 16 stitches = 4 inches. You have decided you want a finished chest measurement of 40 inches (this will be 20 inches across the back and 20 inches across the front).

The pattern calls for 80 stitches across the back.

80 ÷ 16 stitches x 4 inches = 20 inches

If your gauge is off and you are getting 14 stitches over 4 inches you will get the following:

80 ÷ 14 x 4 = 22.85

If you multiply that x 2, to get the chest measurement of your sweater you will see the result is 45.71 inches. More than 5 ½ inches larger than you originally intended.

How Do I Get Gauge

You get gauge by making a gauge swatch using the same yarn you will use in your finished garment. Different patterns will have different types of gauge swatches you need to make.

If you are working in a single stitch type, such as single crochet, then the instructions will say that you need a certain number of stitches and rows over a given number of inches. For example, it might say 15 single crochet stitches and 20 rows over 4 inches.

If it is a more complicated pattern that uses a number of different stitches that form patterns or repeats across the garment then the gauge swatch will consist at least one or two repeats of that pattern so that you can measure it to see if your pattern equals the same number of inches as that given in the pattern.

WHAT IF MY GAUGE DOESN´T MATCH?

If your gauge is off, you simply change the size of your crochet hook. If you have too few stitches per inch, then you need a larger crochet hook to make the stitches a little larger. If you have too many stitches per inch, then you need a slightly smaller crochet hook to make your stitches a little smaller.

Choose a different crochet hook and make a new swatch. It may seem boring, but it will be worth it when you produce a sweater that fits YOU and not fat Uncle Charlie.

CHAPTER 11 – COMMON ABBREVIATIONS AND SYMBOLS

This table shows the common abbreviations used in patterns. If magazines had to write out the words "single crochet" and "double crochet" every time they wanted you to make a single or double crochet their magazines would be very thick. To save paper, they use abbreviations. Below are the most common ones.

If you come across an abbreviation you do not know, check the back of the magazine or pattern leaflet, the abbreviations used should be listed there with their full meanings.

If you get stuck, go online and Google the abbreviation and include the word "crochet" in your search string. For example: What does V-stitch crochet mean?

Some responses will even include videos showing you how to make the V-stitch.

Common Abbreviations in Crochet	
Approx.	Approximately
beg	beginning
bet	between
blp	back loop
bp	back post
cc	contract color
ch	chain
dc	double crochet
dec	decrease(s)(ing)
dtr	double triple crochet
flp	front loop only
foll	following(ing)
fp	front post

hdc	half double crochet
inc	increase(s)(ing)
mc	main color
patt	pattern
rem	remaining
rep	repeat
rib	ribbing
rnd(s)	round(s)
rs	right side
sc	single crochet
sl st	slip stitch
st(s)	stitch(es)
tog	together
tr	triple crochet
ws	wrong side

yo	yarn over/around the hook

STANDARD YARN CHART

Yarn Weight Symbol & Category Names	LACE 0 DENTELLE Liston	SUPER FINE 1 SUPER FIN Super Fino	FINE 2 FIN Fino	LIGHT 3 LÉGER Ligero	MEDIUM 4 MOYEN Medio	BULKY 5 BULKY Abultado	SUPER BULKY 6 TRÈS ÉPAIS Super Abultado	JUMBO 7 GÉANT Jumbo
Type of Yarns in Category	Fingering 10-count crochet thread	Sock, Fingering, Baby	Sport, Baby	DK, Light Worsted	Worsted, Afghan, Aran	Chunky, Craft, Rug	Super Bulky, Roving	Jumbo, Roving
Knit Gauge Range* in Stockinette Stitch to 4 inches	33–40** sts	27–32 sts	23–26 sts	21–24 sts	16–20 sts	12–15 sts	7–11 sts	6 sts and fewer
Recommended Needle in Metric Size Range	1.5–2.25 mm	2.25–3.25 mm	3.25–3.75 mm	3.75–4.5 mm	4.5–5.5 mm	5.5–8 mm	8–12.75 mm	12.75 mm and larger
Recommended Needle U.S. Size Range	000–1	1 to 3	3 to 5	5 to 7	7 to 9	9 to 11	11 to 17	17 and larger
Crochet Gauge* Ranges in Single Crochet to 4 inch	32–42 double crochets**	21–32 sts	16–20 sts	12–17 sts	11–14 sts	8–11 sts	7–9 sts	6 sts and fewer
Recommended Hook in Metric Size Range	Steel*** 1.6–1.4 mm Regular hook 2.25 mm	2.25–3.5 mm	3.5–4.5 mm	4.5–5.5 mm	5.5–6.5 mm	6.5–9 mm	9–15 mm	15 mm and larger
Recommended Hook U.S. Size Range	Steel*** 6, 7, 8 Regular hook B–1	B–1 to E–4	E–4 to 7	7 to I–9	I–9 to K–10 ½	K–10 ½ to M–13	M–13 to Q	Q and larger

Printed in Great Britain
by Amazon